I Believe in Jesus

*Lovingly dedicated to
my precious grandchildren.*

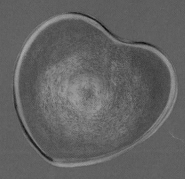

Text copyright © 1999 by John MacArthur
Illustrations copyright © 1999 by Pam Rossi

Published in Nashville, Tennessee, by Tommy Nelson®,
a Division of Thomas Nelson, Inc.

Scripture quotations are from the *International Children's Bible*®,
New Century Version®, © 1983, 1986, 1988, 1999 by Tommy Nelson®,
a Division of Thomas Nelson, Inc.

Library of Congress Cataloging-in-Publication Data

MacArthur, John, 1939–
   I believe in Jesus : leading your child to Christ / by John
MacArthur ; illustrations by Pam Rossi.
     p.   cm.
   ISBN 0-8499-7511-5; ISBN 1-4003-0474-1 (with CD)
   1. Theology, Doctrinal Juvenile literature. 2. Children Prayer—
books and devotions—English. I. Title.
BT77.M12 1999
249—dc21

                                                  99-23599
                                                    CIP

Printed in the United States of America

04 05 06 07 LBM 5 4 3 2 1

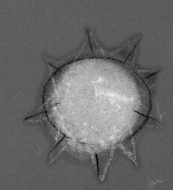

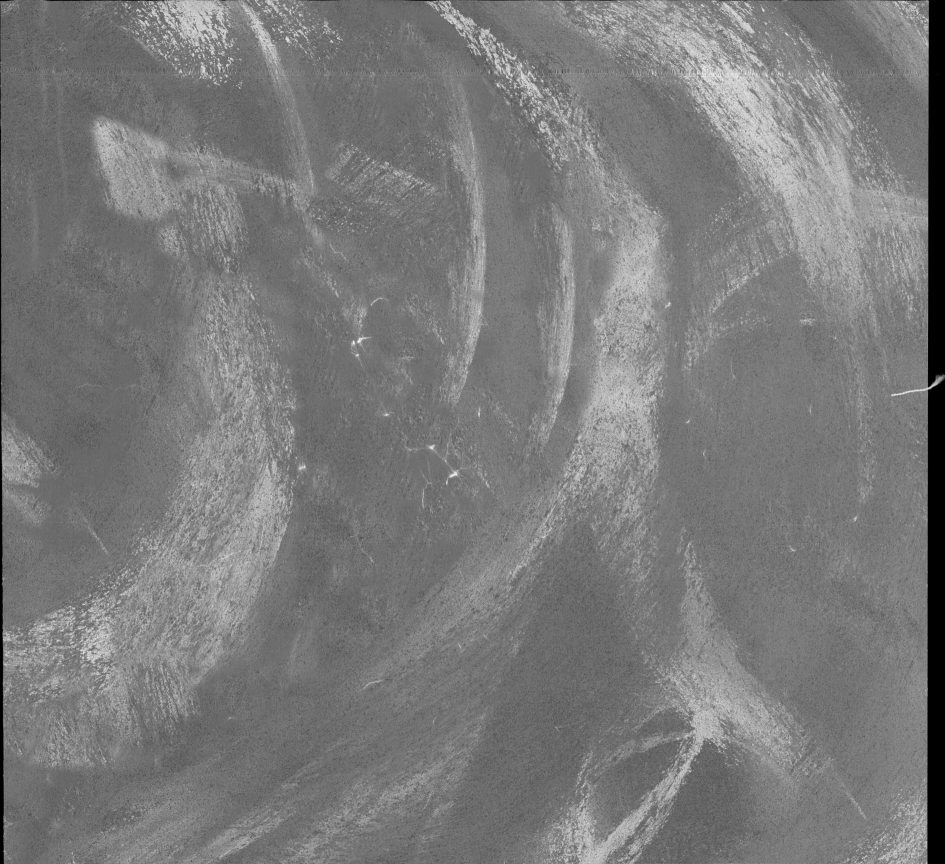

Everything about God is beautiful, good, wise, and perfect. He created angels to live with Him in heaven forever. But some of the angels did not love Him, so God made them leave heaven. God also made the universe with Earth in it. He made the sun and moon and stars. He made the plants and animals and birds and fish. Then He made people.

"In the beginning God created the sky and the earth" (GENESIS 1:1).

". . . your Father in heaven is perfect" (MATTHEW 5:48).

"God makes his angels. . . . All the angels are spirits who serve God and are sent to help those who will receive salvation" (HEBREWS 1:7, 14).

ALSO SEE GENESIS 1:1–2:25; REVELATION 12:8–9.

The first man and woman God created were Adam and Eve. God gave them the beautiful Garden of Eden to live in. But a very sad thing happened. Adam and Eve disobeyed God. They let Satan, one of the bad angels, talk them into doing something God had told them not to do. God punished them by making them leave the garden. Their sins—all the bad things they did—had separated them from God. Every person born since Adam and Eve disobeys God, too. That is why all people die and should go to a place of punishment forever.

"There is no one without sin. None! . . . All people have sinned and are not good enough for God's glory" (ROMANS 3:10, 23).

"When someone sins, he earns what sin pays—death" (ROMANS 6:23).

ALSO SEE GENESIS 3:1–24.

Have you ever noticed how hard it is to always be good, kind, loving, and unselfish? How hard it is to obey? How hard it is to always love God with all your heart? Well, like other people, sometimes you do bad things, too. God could leave you like that and punish you just as He did Adam and Eve and the bad angels. But because God loves people so much, He wants to fill His beautiful heaven with people who will live with Him forever. Our sin should keep us out of heaven, but instead, God invites everyone—you too!—to come to Him and ask for forgiveness for our sins. And He *promises* forgiveness to each one who asks.

"For God loved the world so much that he gave his only Son. God gave his Son so that whoever believes in him may not be lost, but have eternal life" (JOHN 3:16).

ALSO SEE ROMANS 6:23; EPHESIANS 1:7; 1 JOHN 1:9.

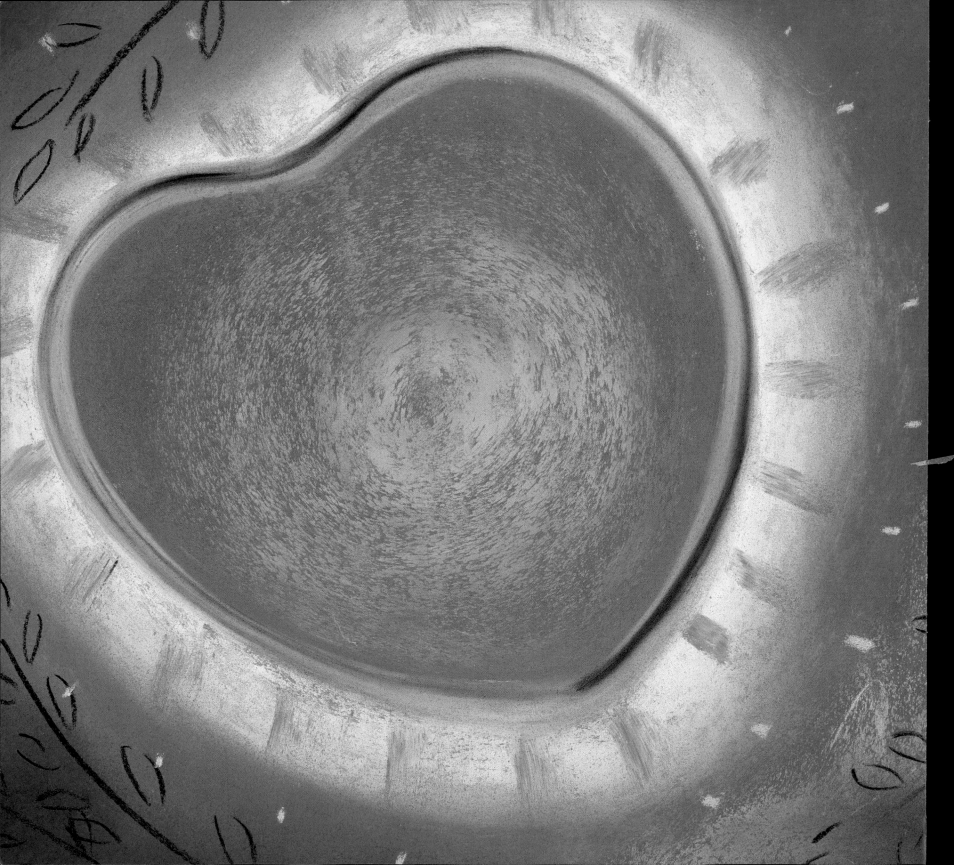

How can God just forgive us? Shouldn't He punish us? If God forgives us, does that mean that the bad things we do are not *really* that bad? No, they are bad! In fact, they are so bad that even though God forgives us and doesn't punish us, He still punishes every one of our sins. How can God punish our sins and not punish us? God always knows exactly what to do. He has a plan.

"Lord, you are kind and forgiving.
You have great love for those who call
to you. Lord, hear my prayer.
Listen when I ask for mercy"
(PSALM 86:5–6).

ALSO SEE PSALM 103:8–18.

God's Son, Jesus, came to Earth to take the punishment for us. Jesus is one of the three persons who are God. And Jesus was willing to come down from heaven to become a real human like we are and to be punished for our sins. Jesus came to Earth as a baby. He was born to Mary and Joseph in a town called Bethlehem. He was born to die for us.

"But he was wounded for the wrong things we did. He was crushed for the evil things we did. The punishment, which made us well, was given to him. And we are healed because of his wounds. . . . The Lord has put on him the punishment for all the evil we have done" (ISAIAH 53:5–6).

ALSO SEE MATTHEW 1:18–2:1; JOHN 19:16–37.

Jesus grew up in a town called Nazareth. He preached about God and God's will. Everywhere Jesus went, He did miracles. He never thought, said, or did anything wrong. He never once displeased God. And He never sinned! Not even once. He did everything right all through His life, and God was totally pleased with Him.

"And a voice spoke from heaven. The voice said, 'This is my Son and I love him. I am very pleased with him'" (MATTHEW 3:17).

ALSO SEE MATTHEW 11:2–5; LUKE 4:14–21; HEBREWS 7:26.

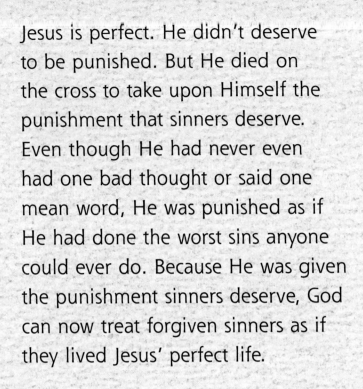

Jesus is perfect. He didn't deserve to be punished. But He died on the cross to take upon Himself the punishment that sinners deserve. Even though He had never even had one bad thought or said one mean word, He was punished as if He had done the worst sins anyone could ever do. Because He was given the punishment sinners deserve, God can now treat forgiven sinners as if they lived Jesus' perfect life.

"Christ died for us while we were still sinners. In this way God shows his great love for us. We have been made right with God by the blood of Christ's death. So through Christ we will surely be saved from God's anger. I mean that while we were God's enemies, God made friends with us through the death of his Son. Surely, now . . . we are God's friends" (ROMANS 5:8–10).

ALSO SEE PHILIPPIANS 3:8–9; COLOSSIANS 3:10.

To complete His plan, God raised Jesus from the dead in three days. Soon after that, Jesus went back to heaven.

The best thing about being forgiven is that we don't have to be punished. Someday we can go to the amazing and wonderful place called heaven. This is a place where everyone is good, happy, loved, and peaceful forever.

You may be thinking, *How can God forgive me like that? Do I have to do something? Will it take a long time for God to forgive me? Do I have to be older?*

"And this was the most important: that Christ died for our sins . . . that he was buried and was raised to life on the third day as the Scriptures say" (1 CORINTHIANS 15:3–4).

ALSO SEE MATTHEW 28:1–10; ACTS 1:9–11; COLOSSIANS 1:3–6; 1 PETER 1:4.

Listen. God will forgive you right now so that you can have a place in heaven. It's His gift! He offers it to you!

Would you like God to forgive you so that someday you can live with Him in heaven? There are two words in the Bible that tell how this gift can be yours.

The first word is BELIEVE. Believe that Jesus alone could die for you and that He died so that God can forgive you for all the bad things you do. Believe that His dying was enough to pay for all your sins. Believe that He came back to life.

"If you use your mouth to say, 'Jesus is Lord,' and if you believe in your heart that God raised Jesus from death, then you will be saved. We believe with our hearts, and so we are made right with God. And we use our mouths to say that we believe, and so we are saved" (ROMANS **10:9–10**).

The second word is RECEIVE. Receive Jesus as your Savior—the perfect One who was punished on the cross for the things sinful people do. That means telling Him you are sorry for the bad things you do. It means thanking Him for dying for sinners like you on the cross. It means telling Him that someday you want to live with Him in heaven with all the forgiven people. Receiving Jesus means telling Him that you want His special gift. You want Him to forgive you!

"But some people did accept him. They believed in him. To them he gave the right to become children of God. They did not become his children in the human way. They were not born because of the desire or wish of some man. They were born of God" (JOHN 1:12–13).

Right now—bow your head. Tell Jesus that you believe in Him and what He did. Tell Him that you want to receive Him as your own Savior. Ask Jesus to forgive you for the times when you disobey. For the times when you are unkind and selfish. For everything you do that makes Him unhappy.

"If we say that we have no sin, we are fooling ourselves, and the truth is not in us. But if we confess our sins, he will forgive our sins. We can trust God. He does what is right. He will make us clean from all the wrongs we have done" (1 JOHN 1:8–9).

"Believe in the Lord Jesus and you will be saved" (ACTS 16:31).

If you asked honestly, you can trust God to forgive you! Keep trusting Him from now on. You show that you accept God's forgiveness by being baptized and obeying His Word.

Jesus will be your friend forever. Someday, He will take you to heaven to live with our amazing God.

"The Father gives me my people. Every one of them will come to me, and I will always accept them. . . . Everyone who sees the Son and believes in him has eternal life" (JOHN 6:37, 40).

ALSO SEE JOHN 14:1–6.

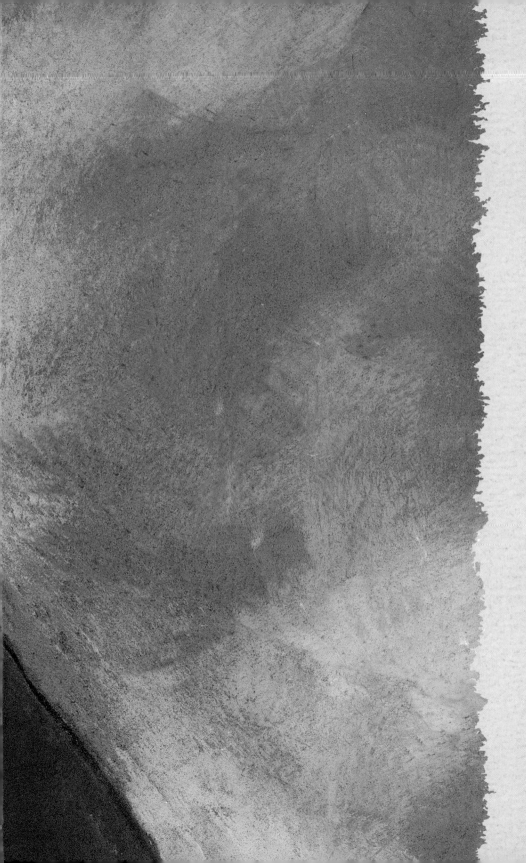

The Holy Spirit is the other of the three who are God. He will come to live inside you and help you to love God. He will help you obey God and praise Him.

"You should know that your body is a temple for the Holy Spirit. The Holy Spirit is in you. You have received the Holy Spirit from God. You do not own yourselves. You were bought by God for a price. So honor God"
(1 CORINTHIANS 6:19–20).

ALSO SEE EPHESIANS 1:13–14.

Tell all your friends the wonderful story of how God forgives people and how He forgave you.

Welcome to God's special family, the Church!

"More and more people were being saved every day; the Lord was adding those people to [the church]" (ACTS 2:47).